Corner Kick **Mapei Football Center, Sassuolo**

A functional tradition
Giancarlo Floridi and Angelo Lunati
10

Modern football, the local and the global: Sassuolo in context
John Foot
21

Catenaccio *als symbolische Form*
Pier Paolo Tamburelli
42

Appendix

Credits
59

Biographies
60

Imprint
60

PARK BOOKS

A functional tradition
Giancarlo Floridi and Angelo Lunati

Questions

Sassuolo is a small town of 40,000 inhabitants, close to Modena, on the Via Aemilia. The training center for its Serie A football club was built on public land through a public-private partnership with the local authority. After 30 years the building will become entirely publicly owned. The center provides training facilities and offices for Sassuolo FC players and staff, as well as a press room and a covered stand for 200 people. Alongside the building, there is a complex of six different football pitches with both artificial and natural turf. The football club trains 20 teams in 20 different leagues, involving around 600 people aged between six and 40.

The project posed a double challenge: first, to understand exactly how a football training center functions, and then to give the building a typological and formal dimension that goes beyond that function. The design attempts to answer a series of concrete questions. What form should a new building take in the landscape? What is the character of a building that goes beyond its function? How do you fulfill the need for representation in such a mediatized sport? Is it possible for a contemporary building to embody the dimension of duration?

Form

The project seeks to mediate between two distinct themes: on the one hand, the suburban situation, with its industrial buildings, warehouses, truck parks and scattered traces of the former agricultural landscape; on the other, the abstract, geometric character of the training grounds, traced in the white lines on the pitches.

The images in Luigi Ghirri's *Esplorazioni sulla Via Aemilia* (Explorations along the Via Aemilia), from the summer of 1986, speak of a territory shaped by the often dramatic, conflictual relationship between past and present, between contemporary and enduring historical conditions. In this context, the photo of the small settlement of Cittanova, a few kilometers from the site of the project, seemed particularly interesting. Cittanova is part of the complex territorial system that has developed over the centuries along the Via Aemilia, with the line of the Roman road generating a network of urban routes and places that define the essential structure of the Po Valley. Ghirri's image on page 7 shows the facade of the church, frontal and orthogonal to the street, which is aligned with the centuriation grid. The facade has an iconic two-dimensional character that is at once simple and monumental. Another Ghirri image from the same book, shown on page 6, shows a football match where the flat landscape merges with the pitch and the strong light on the game gives way to the absolute darkness of the background. The relationship that the new building wants to establish with the territory is, in the same vein, both synthetic and complex, simple and ambiguously monumental. The built volume, which is itself the length of a football pitch, establishes a clear spatial and volumetric relationship with the horizontality and emptiness of the flat landscape. A calm presence visible from a great distance, it forms a distinctive landmark that invests the historical memory of the horizontal system of the agrarian plain with new meaning. Its stepped volume is oriented like a decumanus in the same direction as the abstract centuriation grid, covering what was once agricultural land is now sports fields.

Character and function

A functionalist approach typically results in a mechanical aggregation of the different properties of a building, in which each element is defined by its particular use and expresses its own autonomous values in terms of form and typology, language and materials.

Rejecting that naive desire for a correspondence between form and function, the project seeks a synthetic language that relates to the overall expression of the building, rather than the representation of its individual functions. Its references are therefore historical buildings—traditional sports facilities and agrarian structures—that convey a pragmatic character through their somewhat archetypal forms and their compactness, sobriety, and expression of the structure. Typologically, the training center draws on the linear elements of rural service buildings, such as the porticoed *barchesse* or their Greek and Roman forerunners, which are arranged longitudinally along the edge of fields, with the form being defined in relation to the open space.

The building sits on the ground without a plinth, directly connected to the soil, like its humble agricultural and manufacturing predecessors. Engaging with a tradition, or attempting somehow to invent one, the project uses various forms, types and characters found in historical service buildings: a linear spatial organization, unitary material, repetition of structure and facade as a form of representation, absence of cladding, colors corresponding to the nature of the materials themselves, arches, arcades, a stepped section, pragmatic use of symmetry.

Monumentality and background

If for Pasolini football represents a "basic rite and evasion, the last sacred representation of our time," then the training center represents the most mysterious, most secret part of the preparation of the liturgy. The autonomous form has elements of monumentality, reflecting the building's strong collective role while also expressing the essential representative quality now expected of the headquarters of a football club, especially in Italy. In contrast to the current *slick* representation of football, however, the character of the training center for this provincial club resides more in the sober and unadorned tone of a frugal and poetic place—the backdrop for the build-up to the performance. Any theatricality is left to the match in the stadium.

The absoluteness of the form of the building derives from its placement as the limit between two identical football pitches, and from its dimensions, derived from the space of the game. Its stepped section offers identical and continuous views of both pitches from every point of the building.

Likewise, the regular, longitudinal repetition of a single symmetrical section creates elevations that are practically identical, differentiated in just a few precise ways. The project seeks to form a backdrop that is at once neutral and stimulating. The clarity of its expression, as a single synthetic organism, helps to contain the heterogeneity and vitality of the functions of a complex program.

Just as a football is not round but is more closely related to diverse faceted surfaces than to an ideal sphere, the building does not translate function directly to form, or vice versa. Rather than being the sum of functional elements (like recent suburban expansions), the project is a single building articulated by organizing the functional program vertically in a logical but nonhierarchical sequence (first-team players, youth squads, staff and managers).

Facades

The long facades of the building, with their straight, dark brick surfaces, are intended to assert a strong physical presence in the landscape, one that refers to the Via Aemilia's productive tradition of quality and reserve. This expression of solidity not only reinforces the synthetic quality of the building but also gives it a sober, monumental character appropriate to this rural setting, underpinning the sense of a new collective resource and a "newly invented tradition."

The character of the long facades is consistent with the general scale of the volume: the openings are proportionate to the size and articulation of a sports center, rather than being directly derived from the internal spaces, as in a building with a domestic tone.

Each of the short sides, on the other hand, has a distinct character. While the south end is blank, indifferent to any expressiveness, the north end, which contains the main entrance, forms a shallow curved facade. Its lower part, with an integrated bench, is made of polished precast concrete, while its upper part is of brick, laid in stretcher bond. The shadowing of the protruding rows of brickwork further enhances the ambiguous monumentality of this little facade, resonating with the lack of cladding and harsh beauty of unfinished historical facades like San Lorenzo in Florence or San Petronio in Bologna.

From a distance the building appears as a single mass of the same material: dark gray brick, laid horizontally to accentuate the three different orders of floor height and the regular span of the structure.

Balconies are placed along the facades in accordance with the maximum allowable external surface areas. Their profile is curved to avoid intercepting the building volume, except at a single discreet point.

Matter

On the exterior a dark and hard brick, the same color as the earth, is used to form wall bays as buttresses with a tapering width and to dress the building in a thick masonry skin. Within the uniform grain of the external wall, precast concrete polished architraves act as ornamental friezes marking the main entrances and the openings.

The interior is made of exposed materials corresponding directly to the concrete structures cast in situ and precast as the predalles, like Aldo Rossi's Modena Cemetery not far away, and wall partitions made in concrete bricks.

Flooring throughout is in the same green resin, apart from service areas with green antislip tiles, the gym with its greenish linoleum floor and the wooden raised planks in the offices. The interior, without any further finishing and coating, corresponds to the sobriety and pragmatic character of the exterior.

The internal walls on the perimeter and the main distribution corridors are in white cellular concrete blocks with two finishes: rough and smooth, up to 140 cm in height, left exposed to ensure durability of cleaning and the guarantee of minimum maintenance needed in these lengthy and crowded spaces.

All the metalwork, like balustrades and handrails, are in gray steel, while the windows are in aluminum in its natural color.

The secondary buildings such as the grandstand and the electrical substation are made with reinforced concrete structures and curtain walls in dark gray cellular concrete blocks.

Program

The program of the main building is divided over four floors—three above ground, one below. The ground floor contains the public spaces, including a small auditorium, along with the facilities for the Serie A team, and offers access to the playing fields on either side. The first floor is for the youth squads, while the second floor contains offices and staff meeting rooms. The basement level is for visitor and public use.

Facilities for the Serie A team include: physiotherapy, laser room, gymnasium, changing rooms, toilets, showers, ice bath, relaxation room, coach's office and separate changing rooms for the coaching and other technical staff.

The first-floor spaces for the youth squads contain: physiotherapy with offices, laser room, technical office and locker room, shared toilets, showers, ice bath, dedicated stairway to the pitches, gym, offices for the managers of the youth squad.

The management offices on the second floor are arranged in an extended linear sequence of individual and shared workspaces, meeting rooms and services, providing views from any room onto the playing fields and the landscape.

The basement houses the changing rooms for visiting teams and public use, technical plant, storage spaces, laundry room and hydrotherapy pool.

The covered grandstand building can accommodate up to 200 spectators. Beneath it, there are spaces for storing equipment, public toilets and an indoor area with vending machines. There are no fences dividing the playing fields.

The service building to the north contains an MV/LV transformer substation, a technical room with a generator, a waste room and a bike shed.

Access

The main access to the sports center is from the square to the north, which is connected to the public highway through the concession area on Via Regina Pacis. A second, internal road to the north leads to a public car park. On this north side, two entrances with galvanized steel gates serve both vehicles and pedestrians, while there is a further pedestrian entrance to the south, via the existing car park in the Cà Marta center. The first-team pitch, and the freight elevator for suppliers, are accessed from the east side of the building. On the west side, the pitch is connected to both the youth squad changing rooms on the first floor and the visiting team facilities in the basement.

Access to the first-team, youth and office areas is controlled with respect to the general flows of the building through the atrium and the main staircase. Visitors can access the basement from both the main and the secondary staircase, but not from the rest of the building. For functional reasons, the vertical circulation of the building is divided between two staircases. All floors are served by an elevator and a freight elevator.

Levels

The ceiling height on the ground floor, at 4 m, reflects the representative character of the spaces on this level. At the entrance on the north end of the building, a double-height area contains the reception and access to the small auditorium. Beyond this, the spaces for the first team are served by a 1.8-m-wide glazed corridor that overlooks their dedicated pitch on one side and gives onto a series of atria on the other. The atria vary in shape, depending on the role of the spaces they access, and form part of a central band of service elements that acts as a buffer between the circulation area and the physiotherapy, coach and technical offices, preserving their privacy both visually and acoustically. The first-team changing rooms then constitute an autonomous area, focused around a large oval element, finished in timber, which contains the lockers with benches and service spaces (for linen, tools, and so on). The oval room is set back from the facade both to prevent anyone looking in (as required by Italian Olympic Committee rules) and to ensure the necessary soundproofing. The circulation area within the changing rooms connects the oval room with the relaxation area and the sanitary block with toilets, showers and ice bath. At the south end, the gym extends over the entire width of the building. The structure of the pillars defines a large central space—the teaching area—and lateral bands towards the facades, which become circulation spaces.

The first floor has a ceiling height of 3.4 m. The youth squad area is served by a 1.8-m-wide circulation corridor. On the east side it is extensively glazed and overlooks the first-team pitch. On the west it gives onto the youth squad spaces—changing rooms, offices, physiotherapy, and their own dedicated pitch. At the south end, the gym again extends over the entire width of the building, and this time also incorporates a double-height area. The changing rooms are identical spaces, arranged perpendicular to the corridor, with showers accessible from their long sides. A toilet area common to all the changing rooms (with three cubicles and a common circular channel sink) is located at the stairs leading to the ground floor and the exit to the pitch. All spaces can be accessed through doors in small setbacks along the main corridor. The management offices for the youth squad are located at the main staircase, alongside a small service space and a break area.

On the top floor, the ceiling height is 3 m. This entire floor is the preserve of the management of the sports club, with offices as well as toilets, a server and printer space, a large meeting room and external terraces on both sides of the building. A hatch with a retractable ladder provides maintenance access to the top of the building. The roofs are all flat, with a system of channels for water collection. The ones on the first and second floor span 2 m and are made with a sloping screed, a waterproof membrane and a top layer of dark gravel.

West facade

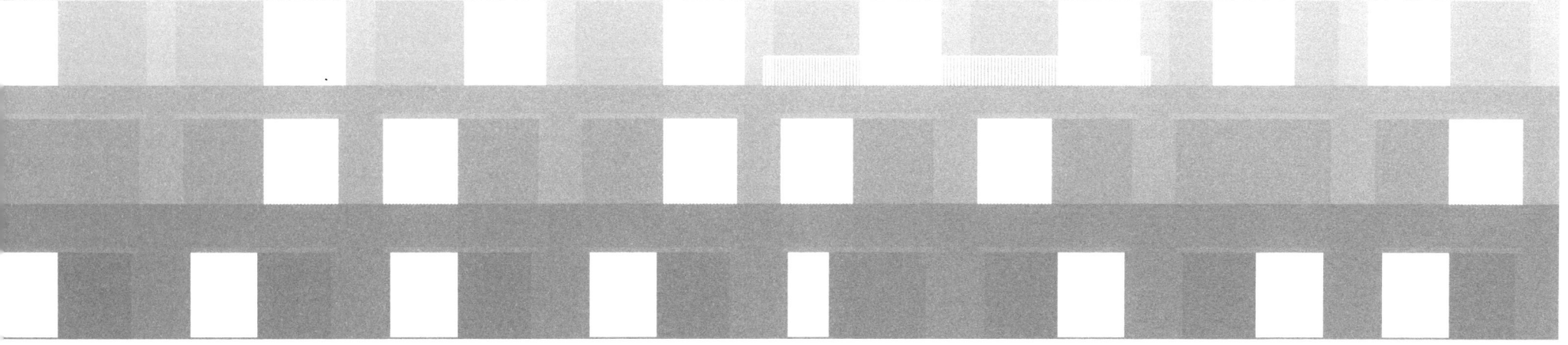

East facade

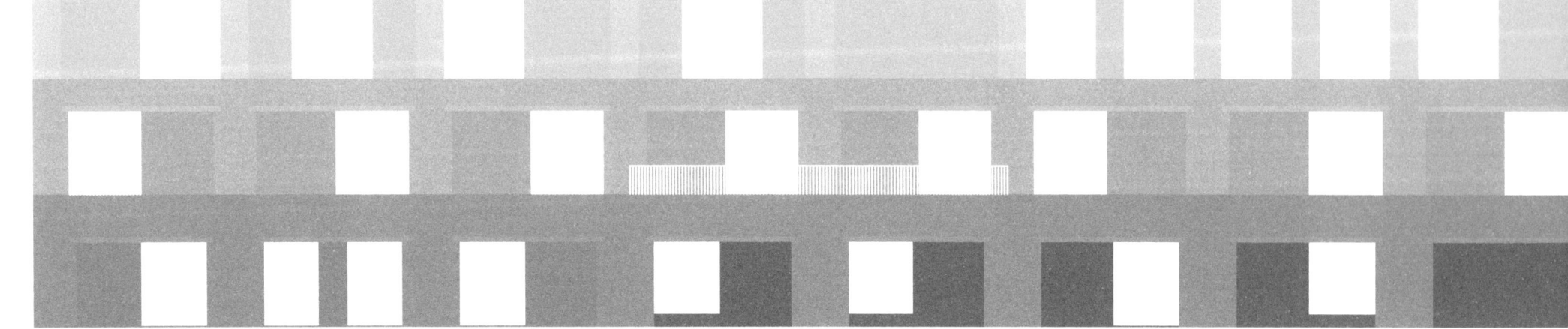

0 1   5   10   15

15

North facade axonometry

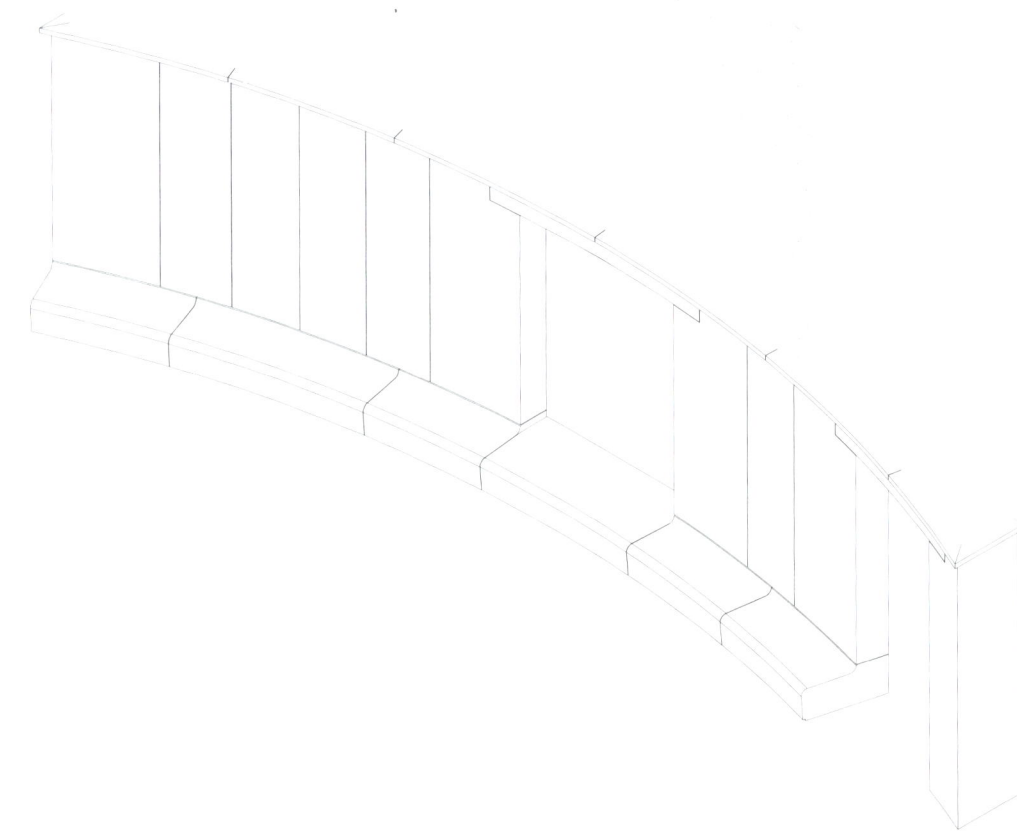

North and south facades

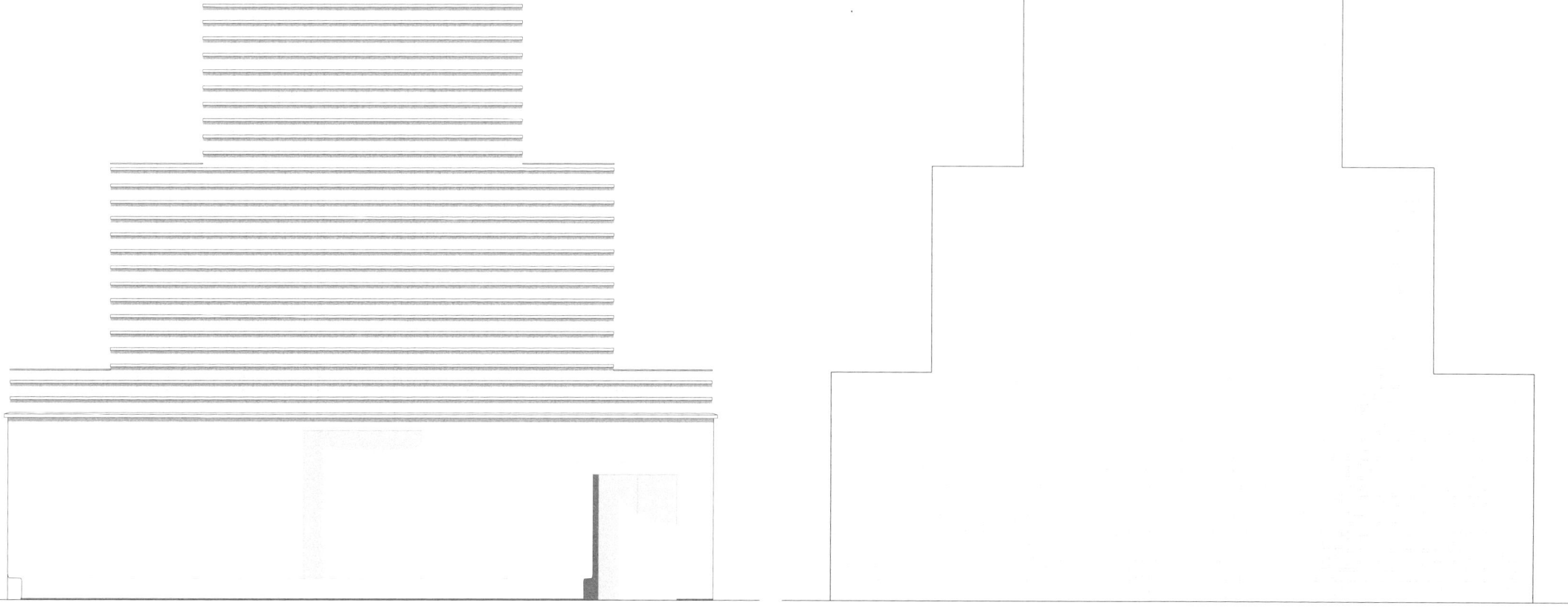

Cross-sections

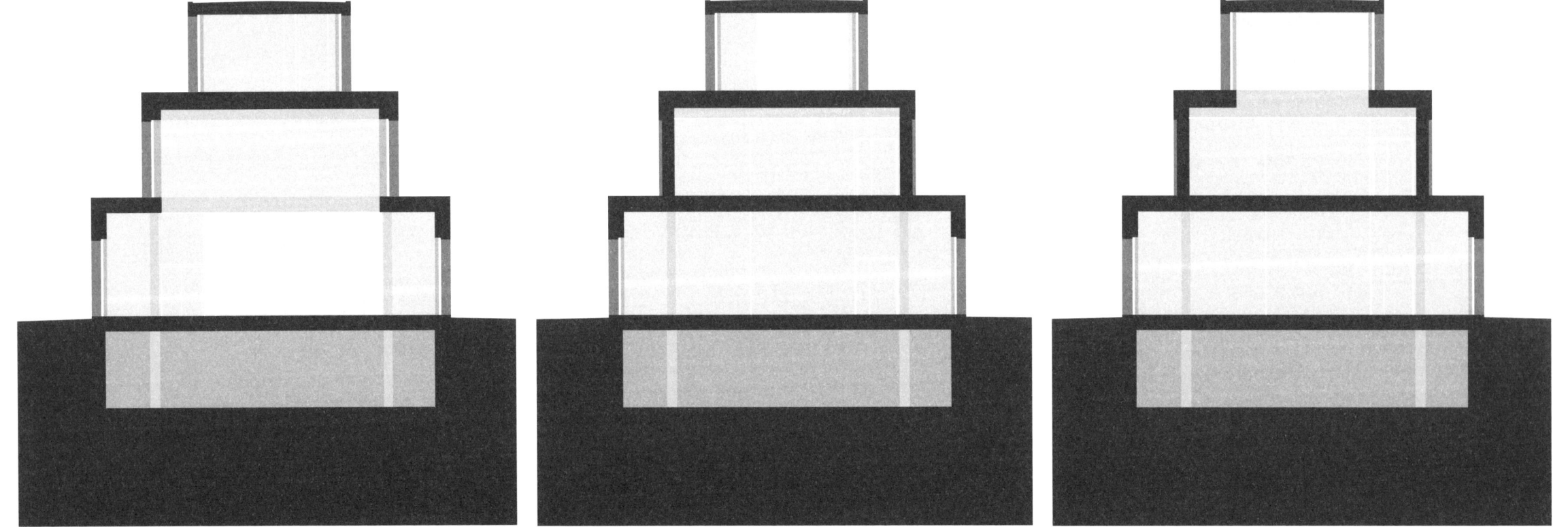

Modern football, the local and the global: Sassuolo in context
John Foot

We are against/Modern football. This is what many fans sing, nowadays, during matches. But what do they mean by "modern football"? Overpaid players, the same rich teams always winning, alienating and expensive stadiums and tickets, clubs detached from their base and their territory, VAR. In many ways these fans are right. Football is global, it is big business, it is usually not played for those in the stadium at all, it is dominated by the huge, bloated, corporate clubs. Games are staged all week, for TV, making the "job" of the faithful fan more and more difficult and expensive.

The old traditions have been swept away—games at 3 p.m. on a Saturday in the UK and on Sundays in Italy. What made football so popular, at first, has been progressively destroyed—the regularity, the mystery, the doubt, the arguments, the religious-like aspects of loyalty, trust and unthinking attachment. Now we know everything, we can see everything, wherever we are, and we can bet on everything, all the time, and talk about it, all the time, on social media. There is no mystery, precious little loyalty, but there is an enormous amount of money involved. Perhaps there is no longer even any history, whatever that means. But sometimes, every so often, something happens to restore faith in this simple game, which just needs a ball, some legs, and a goal. Claudio Ranieri's victory with Leicester City in 2016 was one such moment—something so unlikely, so surprising, that many people still can't even believe it really happened. Months later, as if to confirm the complaints of those fans about modern football, Ranieri was sacked.

The coronavirus crisis has taken this concept of "modern football" to a further level. How could football be played during a pandemic? For a long time, it seemed that it was impossible to do so. This is a contact sport. The fans—even in the modern stadiums—are often pressed together, at touching distance, shouting and jumping up and down, especially in the curva, the part which hates "modern football" the most. But money talks—and there was too much of it involved to stop the games altogether, especially at the higher level.

Some championships stopped altogether—France, for example. But in Italy, and in England, the show went on. Yet, there was no crowd. Fans were not allowed in. Games were played in a ghostly atmosphere, in cavernous buildings with words and sometimes banners laid across the seats with nobody in them. In some places there were even fake fans—and there was more. TV producers realized that the fans were part of the show. Would anyone actually watch a game without fans? What could be done? So a solution was discovered—fake noise. At first this didn't work at all—the noise seemed inappropriate. Yet it got better, more scientific, better suited to the "action" on the pitch. It turned out that perhaps you didn't need those fans at all. Audiences would still watch the product, right across the world. "Modern football" had triumphed. Games could be played at any time, on any day, and linked entirely to the needs of the global public watching on screens in Africa, China and in every single country in the world. There is no other global product created by capitalism that has the power of modern football. In this context, what is the meaning of the local at all—towns, identities, histories, cultures? Do these things even matter any more? Is there any point even thinking about them? Should every club just become a version of every other club, with no roots, no traditions, no connections to the landscape, the territory, the past? Yet there are other examples, other pointers, other directions of travel.

Sassuolo is a small town, famous above all for its ceramic production and—in Italy—for being the birthplace of the singer Caterina Caselli. Sassuolo's football team, the Green and Blacks, was partly formed in 1920 (but only took its present form and name in 1974—as US Sassuolo Calcio). It had never even been in Serie B before 2008, when it won promotion under manager Massimiliano Allegri. Then, something incredible began to take place. The team rose through the divisions, right up to Serie A in 2013, with a last-minute goal against Livorno. And as if this wasn't enough, it began to win games in the top division, qualifying for the Europa League in 2016. Sassuolo has not been mere relegation fodder. The players have tried and succeeded in beating the big teams, and played attacking football. Along the way, there were some memorable moments, such as Domenico Berardi's four goals in a 4–3 defeat of AC Milan, and their first-ever game in Europe.

How has this "miracle" been possible? Much of the credit must go to the businessman Giorgio Squinzi and the Mapei company, who took over the club in 2003 and stayed with it through good and bad times, as well as investing heavily in the infrastructure, and the playing staff. Sassuolo defeated Inter Milan an extraordinary seven times between 2013 and 2020, and every time they won, Squinzi, who supported AC Milan as a boy, would create a new trophy to celebrate. Sassuolo's success is not ephemeral, or even global. The club and its owners have deep roots in their territory and its people. They are creating a legacy which will survive in the hard times, and are not setting up the team for bankruptcy and free fall, as has happened with so many other clubs who managed to make it to Serie A over the years. Squinzi sadly died in October 2019, and the entire squad was present at his funeral in the Duomo di Milano.

A concrete testimony to this sense of rootedness, and the importance of creating real outcomes for the club, linked to the landscape and the city, is this new Mapei Football Center. Designed by architects Giancarlo Floridi and Angelo Lunati plus a team of designers and engineers, is a multi-use space, hosting and catering for all the teams from kids to adults and beyond (and providing them with six pitches). The professionals are not meant to be separated in these spaces, either from the landscape or the general population. This is not a bombastic, over blown building, but quiet, modest, functional and yet elegant. It is modern and sleek, but not part of "modern football," as the fans often see it, and which pays homage to many typical, and exceptional, agricultural, religious and industrial buildings that can be seen across this region, as well as the origins of football itself, and the early stadiums (with the beautiful and almost miniature spectators' stand). In short, this is a new kind of public space, innovative and sustainable, designed to fit in in a whole series of ways and to serve the needs of the squad, its fans and the residents of the area, without the alienating fences and gates which mark so many "modern" grounds these days in Italy. This is a set of buildings which are democratic, open and stylish, but also modest—in line with the role played by US Sassuolo on and off the pitch in the last few years—and with the colours of green and black prominent, yet understated. A fitting legacy to Giorgio Squinzi, who was able to open the center before his untimely death.

In a Covid and post-Covid world, Sassuolo's project provides a counterpoint to the globalized, cold, detached project which is "modern football." By connecting to the locale and the territory—by opening up instead of closing down—by expressing simplicity not corporate distance and hostility—Sassuolo football club has chosen a different route toward the 21st century and beyond.

Longitudinal section

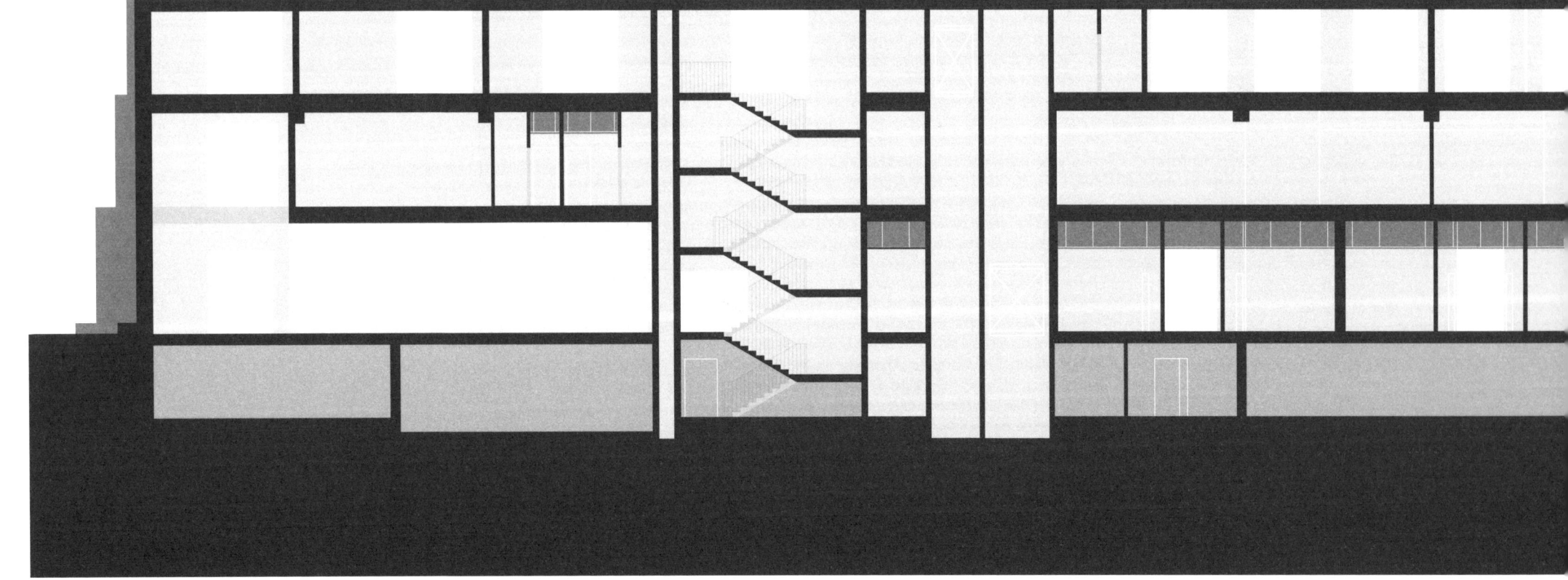

0 1   5   10   15

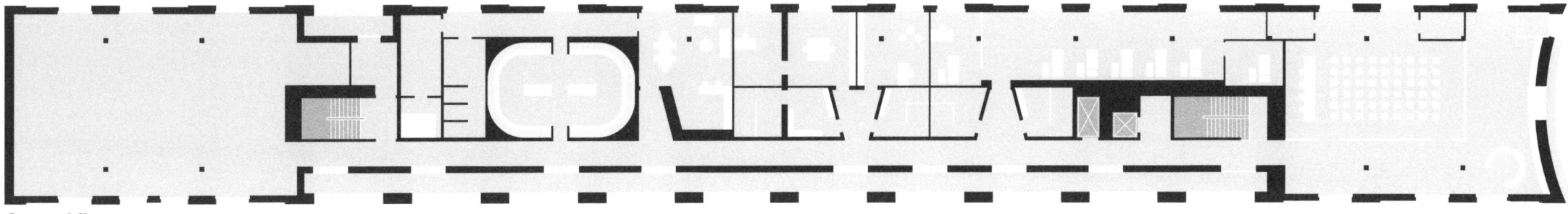
Ground floor

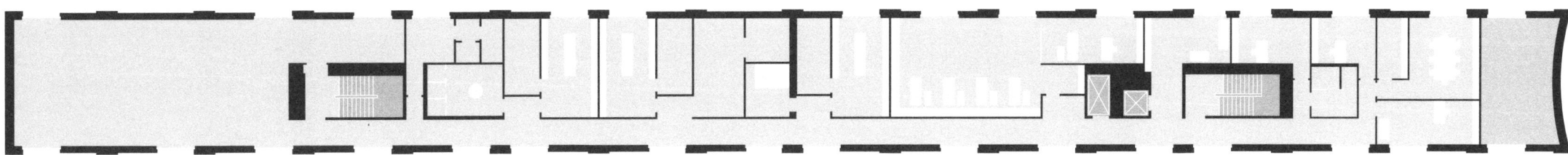
First floor

Second floor

Roof plan

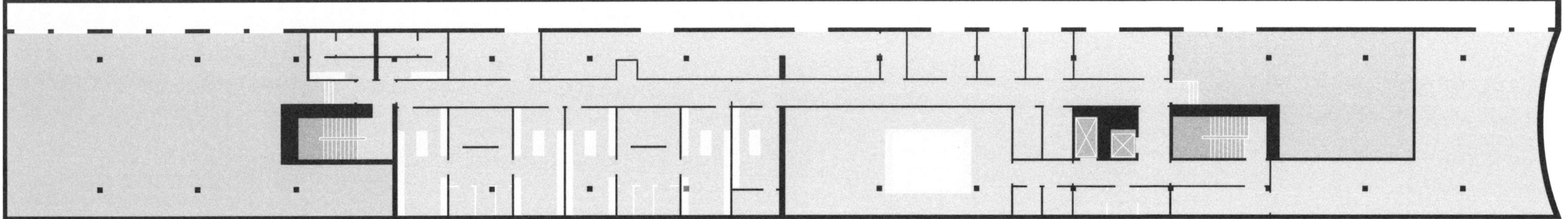
Underground plan

Catenaccio *als symbolische Form*
Pier Paolo Tamburelli

The Chain (*Catenaccio*) is a tactical system in football. In theory, it's only a matter of placing a "free" player behind the backline defense. The Chain has a long history, which begins in Geneva (at Servette), passes through Viani's Salernitana and Rocco's Padova, and has its golden age with Herrera's Internazionale. Actually, rather than a tactical system, The Chain is more of a symbolic form (if not just an attitude of the Italian masses, as highlighted by Gianni Brera). The *Catenaccio* is the manifestation in football of a rural, plebeian and conservative culture, aggravated by the fact that this culture is fully self-aware, and therefore rather sophisticated. This is why Italians, from the crudest to the most refined, have always identified with The Chain, with its immediate declaration of inferiority, with its blind faith in paradoxes. The glory of The Chain isn't the presumed "supremacy of defense" (this was Clausewitz, not Nereo Rocco), nor is it the demented and fanatic need to win at all costs. It's the faith in the psychological disaster, the cruel irony of its method, the very catholic contempt for merit, where nothing is more ridiculous than:

a team (…) that, in order to score, must always play by the book, in perfect form.[1]

The Chain is therefore a mindset (an antilogic) and, most of all, an aesthetic. A down to earth, archaic, plebeian aesthetic, while also rational, comical, mocking. This logic and this aesthetic inspire the whole history of Italian football. One can adhere to it with the fury of Dante and Pasolini or with the detachment of Svevo and Rossini, but nobody can count themselves out.

Mapei Football Center

The Mapei Football Center welcomes the players with a subtle stepped facade, slightly bent, almost entirely without windows. The facade is in very dark brick, which seems to have been baked in the earth's core. The wall in the lobby is clad in a series of giant slabs of prefabricated concrete and perforated by a giant window. The door is on the far right. From here, one can enter and access every function of the building from a central corridor. Visitors are only presented with the *much* shorter side of the Mapei sports center. If the facade is 14 meters at its base, the long side of the building extends along the entire length of the adjoining football field, some 112 meters. Thus, the building ends up being a literal act of measurement. The ruler is placed directly alongside the field, like the disproportionate compass placed on the Palatine in the *Pianta Topografica del Circo Massimo* by Piranesi (*Della Magnificenza*, 1761–65, XXXVI). The building spans a slice of plains appropriated from farmland and destined for use by the football industry. This territorial discipline defines the entire look of the building that doesn't grant itself any exceptions (except the slight baroque curve of the facade, that welcomes arrivals with a courteous nod). The building is three stories, and narrows as the height increases. This creates a stepped section, symmetrical on two sides and with a vaguely Gothic look, almost like a little house stolen from a pharmacist in Lübeck and abandoned at the margins of Modena's *Bassa*. The building is a constant section, a stepped bar stretching along the pitch like bleachers for giants. The essential and vaguely infantile geometry is reminiscent of some early modernist experiments (the Grand Hotel Babylon and Adolf Loos' Scheu house, or Hans Kollhoff's wonderful kindergarten in Frankfurt). The object is mysterious. Its link to football, and more generally to sport, remains obscure. There's nothing muscular, the structure doesn't imitate the activity it houses in any way.

Primo non prenderle (first rule: don't be defeated)

Giancarlo Floridi and Angelo Lunati chose their playing field immediately. "Onsitestudio" is their office, and they are *on site*, with their feet firmly on the ground. This choice of positioning implies a very precise idea of architecture. For Onsitestudio, architecture is architecture, there are no big discoveries to be made, there is no groundbreaking news to wait for. Building is an ancient practice, based on ancient knowledge that there is no need to escape from. Architecture already exists, a heritage to apply and expand, but, most of all, to not wear out. Onsitestudio approaches the discipline with a defensive attitude, prioritizing the protection of architectural knowledge.

This resolute defensive stance isn't proclaimed in aggressive manifestos or noisily propagandized; rather, it defines project activities that are developed with time and care, discovering every new opportunity for a touch-up or a clarification. Every project is an occasion to confirm that architecture can solve even that problem, that understanding this rich tradition is all it takes to see its fruits. The hotel in Piazza Duca d'Aosta shows us that there is a repertoire from which we can deduce models that can be seamlessly integrated into contemporary cities. The Mameli barracks shows us that it's possible to reuse the forms of historic cities to imagine contemporary residences. The transformation of the finance ministry in Rome's EUR highlights a way to change cities without having to start from scratch. The pillars of the Pirelli Learning Center demonstrate that the elegance of high craftsmanship can be preserved. The conservatism of Onsitestudio is limited to this reasonable objective: to not waste resources that are still available, to not miss opportunities, to not ignore the material knowledge that is still sufficiently diffused in contemporary *Lombardy*. It's a toned-down conservatism that is in no way ideological (the ground upon which Onsitestudio is firmly planted certainly doesn't proclaim Carl Schmitt's gloomy laws) and is limited to observing the world with a certain detachment from fashion and with an explicitly adult taste. Its a solidly progressive conservatism, that goes from Piermarini to Boito, to Muzio, to Rogers, to Gregotti, to Zucchi.

What past? What future?

Onsitestudio doesn't want to astonish, it only wants to proceed intelligently, so it has chosen a precise idea of the past and an equally precise idea of the future. This idea of the past, which is also immediately an idea of the future, corresponds with a carefully selected tradition. The construction of this operative memory is less immediate than it may initially seem, and was developed by balancing the rights of a private memory with the duties of a public memory. Belonging to a tradition requires an adhesion, even to episodes that don't conjure up enthusiasm, and involves responsibility for the future of this tradition. Thus, the past Onsitestudio has built for itself is rather complex. On one hand it is made of a *loved tradition*, and on the other by a *respected tradition*.[2] The loved architects are Albini, Asnago and Vender, De la Sota, Jacobsen, Lewerentz, Loos, Nash, Perret, Poelzig, Siza, Tavora, and some more eccentric names such as Andreani, Bindesbøll, or Fisac. Onsitestudio loves their elegance, their civility, the good sense of effective and pertinent urban hypotheses, the beauty of pleasant and complete objects, the capacity to do one's job without feeling forced to hide the love for the design of marble slabs, for the definition of the curve of a banister. Then, there are respected architects, those that cannot be ignored but are definitely more bitter: Diener, Gregotti, Koolhaas, Schinkel, even Rossi, Ernesto Rogers, Ungers. A more sour tradition, even explicitly unpleasant at times, that is nevertheless indispensable to navigate the inevitable hardships of the city. So, ideology, which was initially abandoned, reappears as an intrinsic quality of world history, and therefore impossible to abandon for anyone who isn't blind. Onsitestudio is respectful and skeptical of this world, almost choosing not to explore its more hostile regions, but recognizing that someone must undertake this thankless job. From this recognition without sympathy comes a cautious and mature attitude toward the city, and every transformation is evaluated with extreme care. There is no space for provocations, as our sense of duty always prevails on our eagerness to experiment. The compromise between these two traditions corresponds to the attitude of *professionismo colto* (cultured professionalism), the legendary Milanese creature that almost certainly doesn't exist, but to which Onsitestudio is enthusiastically, uncontrollably dedicated.

Professionismo colto (cultured professionalism)

Cultured professionalism is a label used to describe the production of a group of post-war Milanese architects. It suggests that the work of Asnago and Vender, Caccia Dominioni, Minoletti, and Mangiarotti consisted of a tone rather than a style, one that was in tune with the taste and the ethics of the post-war Milanese ruling class. This group of "cultured professionals" seems to occupy a mid-ground between the explicit political and intellectual work of Albini, BBPR, Figini and Pollini, and Gardella, and the bold-faced pragmatism of the "uncultured professionals" that were only interested in profiting from property speculation. This category, at least starting from Cino Zucchi's book[3] on the work of Mario Asnago and Claudio Vender, has been successful in Europe, and has contributed to defining a model of the Milanese architect that became ever more seductive as the elegance and sobriety of its clients, the bourgeoisie, progressively vanished.

Onsitestudio fervently dedicates itself to this fundamentally extinct category, imagining its work in an ideal and idealized Milan and submitting itself to a professional ethic that is as rigorous as it is knowingly outdated. The theoretical basis for this "exalted cultured professionalism" is elaborated in a series of academic studies, the most explicit of which is perhaps Angelo Lunati's doctorate thesis for the Zurich Polytechnic: *Ideas of Ambiente: History and Bourgeois Ethics in the Construction of Modern Milan, 1881–1969.*[4] Onsitestudio's loyalty to this idea of architecture not only gives their work a certain charm, it also clearly distinguishes it from the work of other contemporary Milanese and European architects. Onsitestudio doesn't share the sad fate of other Milanese studios that were forced to specialize in commercial building, in luxury objects, or to recycle themselves as experts in charity or sustainability. It remains loyal to a hypothesis of architecture that still tries to unite high-quality craftsmanship with a coherent idea of urban design. On the one hand, this means opposition to the fetishization of the rare piece, opposition to the idolatry of the object of affection chosen by the sovereign arrogance of the aesthete. On the other, it means subtracting oneself from pure economic calculations and especially from the commercial sensationalizing of buildings. This work hypothesis isn't just rare in Milan, it's also hard to find in Europe. Onsitestudio's contemporaries have mostly taken a different path, passing from academies to biennials, publishing a lot and building very little, adhering more closely to the strict pillars of the avant-garde. The studio, therefore, has built a very different repertoire: no pavilions, fairs, installations. Rather, hotels, sports centers, houses, offices.

Architecture as a job

The sturdiness of Onsitestudio's buildings comes from this way of understanding the work. Onsitestudio's path is once again a compromise between the ever-growing luxury industry cult of artisanal production and the nonchalance that characterized the production of Italian architects like Rossi, Aymonino and Gregotti. It shows us that a reasonable middle ground is possible, following the example of the postwar architects of Milan. This care is evident from the very first stages of a project, as can be seen from the Place Rogier hotel in Brussels, and corresponds to a precise duty to the city.

Onsitestudio is dedicated to the creation of a deliberately *continuous* city, where the buildings are fundamentally elements of transition between neighboring environments. It is a *flat* city, without a desire to break away, without excessive monumental intentions, where all disciplinary knowledge is invested in building the background. The infinitely controversy-hating muse of Onsitestudio produces a refined yet modest city, benefiting from the symbolic investments that have already been made and confident that it can bring them to the future. This attitude of constantly being rooted in the past corresponds to a precise image of the future: it seems that it may be possible to imagine a relationship between the cities where we have lived and those in which we will live; it seems possible that the buildings we produce may last in time, without having to scrap them every 30 years. Onsitestudio seems optimistic about our cities: we can think of a solid city, sustainable because it can last, can adapt to different scenarios and therefore share and measure the evolution of human life. This deliberately slow city seems to be able to fit our lives, accepting even frenetic moments with gentleness and showing us that it may be possible to live civilly in the future.

1. G. Brera, coverage of FC Internazionale vs. AC Milan, 6–5, November 6, 1949, from *Gazzetta dello Sport*, November 7, 1949.
2. T. S. Eliot, *Tradition and the Individual Talent* (1919), in T. S. Eliot, *The Sacred Wood*, New York: Dover, 1998, pp. 27–33.
3. C. Zucchi, F. Cadeo, M. Lattuada, *Asnago e Vender. Architetture e progetti 1925–1970*, Milan: Skira, 1999.
4. A. Lunati, *Ideas of Ambiente: History and Bourgeois Ethics in the Construction of Modern Milan, 1881–1969*, Zurich: Park Books, 2020.

PRIMA SQUADRA
ASCENSORE
MONTACARICHI

Situation plan

Credits

Location
Via Regina Pacis, 41049 Sassuolo (MO), Italy

Client
US Sassuolo Calcio Spa

Design phase

Architectural design
Onsitestudio srl

Project team
Angelo Lunati, Giancarlo Floridi
Project architects: Cesare Galligani, Paolo Volpetti, Marco Fancelli, Nicolò de Paoli, Veronica Lazzaro, Davide Macchi, Pietro Manazza, Michele Miserotti

Structural project
Milan Ingegneria srl
Ing. Maurizio Milan, Ing. Giovanni Molteni, Ing. Marco Lettieri

MEP
Deerns Italia spa
Ing. Giovanni Consonni, Ing. Giuseppe Dibari, Ing, Riccardo Diaferia,
Ing. Davide Bonetto, Ing. Angelo Pollace

Fire prevention
AFC srl
Ing. Antonio Corbo

Landscape design
Studio Giorgetta Architetti Paesaggisti

Sport facilities consultant
Dott. Agr. Giovanni Castelli
Mapei Sport: Dott. Ermanno Rampinini
Mapei Spa: Ing. Elisa Portigliatti

Facade consultant
Tecnion Consulting
Ing. Riccardo Morasso

LEED consultant
Politecnica Ingegneria ed Architettura
Ing. Ferdinando Sarno

Images
Mammutlab
Arch. Andrea Romano
Emaviz.
Arch. Eugenio Matteazzi

Photography
Stefano Graziani
Filippo Romano
Onsitestudio

Maquette
Stefano Prina

Construction phase

Artistic supervision
Onsitestudio srl

Project team
Angelo Lunati, Giancarlo Floridi
Cesare Galligani, Paolo Volpetti

Direction of the works
Milan Ingegneria srl
Ing. Maurizio Milan, Ing. Sergio Ferrero

MEP construction supervision
United Consulting
Ing. Stefano Colombo, Ing. Eduardo Nievas,
Ing. Diego Nebiolo

Fire prevention
Politecnica Ingegneria ed Architettura
Ing. Massimo Cavazzuti

LEED consultant
Politecnica Ingegneria ed Architettura
Ing. Ferdinando Sarno

General contractor
Colombo Costruzioni Spa

Project management
Mapei Spa
Arch. Elena Beretta

Products, solutions and systems
Mapei Group

Image credits

We are grateful to Archivio Luigi Ghirri and Eredi di Luigi Ghirri for the photographs on pages 6 and 7.

Luigi Ghirri, Cittanova, 1985
Luigi Ghirri, Via Aemilia, 1985
© Eredi di Luigi Ghirri

Stefano Graziani pages:
9, 19, 32, 39, 40, 42, 43, 54, 55, 53, 64

Filippo Romano pages:
4, 5, 6, 7, 8, 10, 11, 18, 20, 28, 29, 30, 31, 33, 34, 35, 36, 37, 38, 41, 46, 47, 48, 49, 50, 51, 52, 56, 57, 58, 59

Delfino Sisto Legnani page: 61

Onsitestudio

Onsitestudio is an architectural practice founded in Milan in 2011, headed by Angelo Lunati and Giancarlo Floridi. Onsitestudio believes in a close relationship between culture and professionalism, also by its teaching at the School of Architecture and research at DAStU, Politecnico di Milano. Among the studio's recent achievements are the hotel building in Piazza Duca d'Aosta, the cultural center BASE and the Pirelli Learning Center in Milan, the new Hotel Palace in Brussels, the Manifattura Tabacchi masterplan for social housing in Piacenza and the BEIC European library in Milan. Onsitestudio's works have been internationally exhibited, widely published and collected in a monograph book published by Quart Verlag. In 2020 Onsitestudio was selected by the architecture magazine *Domus* to feature among the world's 50 most innovative practices.

Giancarlo Floridi (Modena, 1973) graduated from Politecnico di Milano in 1999, studied mainly at Escuela Tecnica Superior de Arquitectura de Madrid and received a PhD at Politecnico di Milano in 2005. He carries out research at DAStU, Politecnico di Milano, and teaching activities as Adjunct Professor at Politecnico di Milano since 2010 and Visiting Professor at IUAV in 2014 and 2021, GSD Harvard 2022.

Angelo Lunati (Milan, 1973) graduated from Politecnico di Milano in 1998, studied also at Facultade de Arquitectura do Porto and received a PhD at ETH Zurich in 2018. He carries out research at DAStU, Politecnico di Milano and teaching activities as Adjunct Professor at Politecnico di Milano since 2010 and Visiting Professor at IUAV in 2014 and 2021, TU WIEN 2021–2022, GSD Harvard 2022.

Pier Paolo Tamburelli

Pier Paolo Tamburelli (Tortona, 1976) studied at the University of Genoa and at the Berlage Institute Rotterdam. In 2004 Tamburelli founded Baukuh together with Paolo Carpi, Silvia Lupi, Vittorio Pizzigoni, Giacomo Summa, and Andrea Zanderigo. Baukuh completed the House of Memory in Milan, the entrance pavilion of the Poretti Brewery in Induno Olona, and is currently developing the restoration of the Seminar School in Hoogstraten, the strategic plan for the Student City of Tirana and the new headquarters of the Albanian Police in Tirana. Baukuh's work has been presented at the Chicago (2017), Rotterdam (2007 and 2011) and Venice biennales (2008 and 2012). Baukuh has been awarded the Idea Tops Award Shenzhen for the Best Public Building of 2016, the honourable mention of the Fritz Höger Preis (2017), was nominated for the Mies van der Rohe Award (2017), the Golden Medal of Italian Architecture (2016 and 2012), and was listed among the *Domus* 50 Best Architecture Firms 2020. Tamburelli has taught at the Berlage Institute Rotterdam, at TUM Munich, at FAUP Porto, at Harvard GSD, at the University of Illinois at Chicago, at TU Vienna, and he is currently a professor at the Milan Politecnico.

John Foot

John Foot is Professor of Modern Italian History in the Department of Italian, University of Bristol. He has published numerous books and articles on Italian history, politics and culture. His recent publications include *The Archipelago: Italy Since 1945* (Bloomsbury, 2019), translated as *L'Italia e le sue storie. 1945–2019* (Laterza), and *Calcio: A History of Italian Football* (Harper, 2010) which came out in Italian as *Calcio. 1898–2010. Storia dello sport che ha fatto l'Italia* (Rizzoli, 2011).

Filippo Romano

Born in 1968, Filippo Romano studied at *ISIA* in Urbino, and specialized at the International Center of Photography ICP in New York; he currently lives and works in Milan. He focuses on architecture and cities. He has published in *Abitare*, *Domus*, *The Plan*, *Rivista Studio*. In June 2006 he realized, together with Emanuele Piccardo, a photographic project on Paolo Soleri which became the book *Soleritown*. In 2007 he won the Pesaresi/Contrasto prize with the photographic project "OFF China." In 2010 and 2014 he exhibited at the Venice Biennale of Architecture. In 2014 he exhibited at the Canadian Center of Architecture the project "Found in Translation," curated by historian Guido Beltramini, about the Palladian influence in the architecture of Thomas Jefferson. He teaches photography on the master of photography program at IUAV in Venice. He has documented the construction of Herzog & De Meuron's architectural project for the new headquarters of the Foundation "Giangiacomo Feltrinelli" in Milan. In 2019 he was one of the photographers of the "Amare l'architettura" exhibition about Gio Ponti at MAXXI in Rome. In May 2021, the "Strada 106" project was displayed in the Italian pavilion at the Biennale of Architecture.

Stefano Graziani

Active at the crossroads between photography, art and architecture, Stefano Graziani contributes with an unconventional voice to the contemporary artistic discourse. His photos have been exhibited internationally by institutions such as Fondazione Prada in Milan, the Venice Biennale of Architecture and the European Art Biennial Manifesta. His work has been extensively published in monographic and collective publications, and he has also personally authored and edited several book projects. Public and private collections such as CCA Montreal, Fondazione Prada in Milan, Maxxi in Rome, Fondazione Fotografia in Modena have acquired his work. He currently teaches photography at IUAV University in Venice as well as at the ISIA in Urbino and NABA in Milan.

Imprint

Editing: Onsitestudio, Giancarlo Floridi, Angelo Lunati
Concept: Samuel Bänziger, Rosario Florio, Larissa Kasper
Translation: Stefano Longobardi
Copy editing: OS, Pamela Johnston
Proofreading English: Colette Forder
Design: Samuel Bänziger, Rosario Florio, Larissa Kasper
Image processing: Marjeta Morinc
Printing and binding: DZA Druckerei zu Altenburg GmbH, Thuringia

© 2023 Onsitestudio and Park Books AG, Zürich

© for the texts: the authors
© for the images: the artists

Park Books
Niederdorfstrasse 54
8001 Zürich
Switzerland
www.park-books.com

Park Books is being supported by the Federal Office of Culture with a general subsidy for the years 2021–2024.

All rights reserved; no part of this publication may be reproduced, stored in a retrieval system or transmitted in any form or by any means, electronic, mechanical, photocopying, recording, or otherwise, without the prior written consent of the publisher.

ISBN 978-3-03860-310-8